はじめに

CONNECTION シリーズは、読みやすさと使いやすさが特長のロングセラー Weaving It Together: Connecting Reading and Writing（Heinle / Cengage Learning）のリーディングパートのみを扱い、15章構成とし、日本の授業で使いやすいよう編集したものです。本書はそのBook 2 のJapan Edition になります。

本書の特徴

本書は、様々な分野から厳選されたトピックの読み物と、英語の文構造およびパラグラフの基本を段階的に学ぶ練習問題から構成されています。読み物には、ロボットが人間の生活を便利にする可能性、人の骨格が表す性格、稲妻の脅威から身を守る方法、右脳と左脳が持つ能力の違い、アメリカの児童の労働、ユニークなペルシャの正月など興味深いものばかりでなく、心温まる民話が一篇、じっくり味わえる有名詩人の短詩も一篇あります。英文は450語〜500語前後の長さになっています。初見のものでもある程度の速さで読めるようになるために、本書では、（1）（辞書を使わずに速読するのは、語数が多くなるにつれ難しくなりますから）辞書を使ってもいいので、なるべく日本語を介さずに読み進める、（2）わからない単語はできる限りで構わないので、文脈から推測する、（3）本文の主旨、大意を把握しながら読む、という練習を提供します。これらのスキルを身につけることにより、さらに上級のあらゆるジャンルの読み物を読みこなせるリーディング力が養成されます。

本書の構成

Pre-Reading Activity

本文を読み始める前に、各章冒頭にある写真やイラストを見ながら、トピックに関するスキーマ（予備知識）を活性化させ、理解を助けるためのディスカッションを行ないます。あまりなじみのないトピックの場合は、ペアやグループで情報交換、意見交換をしてみましょう。

Vocabulary Exercise

本文を読み終えたら、文中に使われた語彙の理解度をチェックします。適切な単語を選んで、与えられた文を完成させるタイプの問題です。わからない単語に遭遇したときは、前後の文脈から意味を推測してみましょう。その後、本文下の英英注で語彙の意味を確認してください。それでも意味がわからない場合は、後で必ず英和辞典で確認しておきましょう。

Comprehension Exercise

本文を読み終えたら、main idea（主旨）とdetails（詳細情報）の理解度をチェックします。本文のmain ideaを把握する際には、全体を通して何を言わんとしているのかを考えてみましょう。特定の詳細情報を探すときには、必要な箇所だけを読むscanning（拾い読み）をしてみましょう。

Discussion

語彙の意味と本文の理解度のチェックが終わったら、本文でとり上げられたトピックについて考えをまとめてみましょう。適宜、ペア、グループ、またはクラスで自由に意見交換をしてみて下さい。

編著者

2014年秋

□本書の語注については、下記を参考にしております。
英英脚注：*Oxford Advanced Learner's Dictionary*, 6th edition（Oxford University Press）
英日後註：*Random House English Japanese Dictionary*, 2nd edition（小学館）

2 — Pre-Intermediate Level
CONTENTS

Unit title [The number of words of reading passage] Page

Unit	Title	Page
Unit 1	Robots [525 words]	1
Unit 2	The Shape of the Face [584 words]	7
Unit 3	Killer Bees [519 words]	13
Unit 4	Celebrating Fifteen [492 words]	19
Unit 5	A Folktale [491 words]	25
Unit 6	Lightning [537 words]	31
Unit 7	Potatoes [515 words]	37
Unit 8	Right Brain or Left Brain? [532 words]	43
Unit 9	Louis Braille [529 words]	49
Unit 10	Laws about Children [580 words]	55
Unit 11	The World's Most Unusual Millionaire [492 words]	61
Unit 12	Delicacies [524 words]	67
Unit 13	Corn Flakes [636 words]	73
Unit 14	The Persian New Year [560 words]	79
Unit 15	A Poem [28 words]	85
Supplemental Notes		**89**

CONNECTION 2 Pre-Intermediate Level

Weaving It Together: Connecting Reading and Writing
Book 2 / Second Edition
Milada Broukal

Copyright © 2004 by Heinle, a part of Cengage Learning

CENGAGE Learning CENGAGE™ Learning logo is a trademark under license.

This authorized adaptation was published by Shohakusha 2006, 2015.
ALL RIGHTS RESERVED. No parts of this book may be reproduced or transmitted in any form or by any means, electronic or mechanical, including photocopying, recording, or any information storage and retrieval system, without permission in writing from the Publisher.

Unit 1 Robots

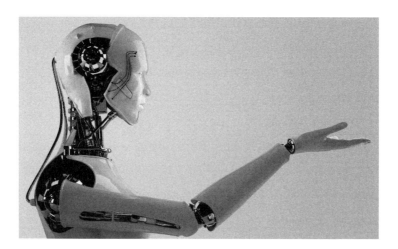

✓ Pre-Reading Activity

Discuss these questions.

1. What kinds of things would you like to have a robot do for you?

   _____

2. How can a robot be useful in a school?

   _____

Reading

Robots are smart. With their computer brains, they can do work that humans prefer not to do because it is dangerous, dirty, or boring. Some robots are taking jobs away from people. Bobby is a mail carrier robot that brings mail to a large office building in Washington, D.C. There are hundreds of mail carrier robots in the United States. In more than seventy hospitals around the world, robots called Help Mates take medicine down halls, call for elevators, and deliver meals. In Washington, D.C., a tour guide at the Smithsonian museum is a robot called Minerva. About 20 percent of the people who met Minerva said that she seemed as intelligent as a person.

There is even a robot that is a teacher. Mr. Leachim is a fourth-grade teacher robot. He weighs 200 pounds, is six feet tall, and has some advantages as a teacher. One advantage is that he doesn't forget details. He knows each child's name, the parents' names, and what each child knows and needs to know. In addition, he knows each child's pets and hobbies. Mr. Leachim doesn't make mistakes. Each child tells Mr. Leachim his or her name and then enters an identification number. His computer brain puts the child's voice and number together. He identifies the child with no mistakes. Then he starts the lesson.

Another advantage is that Mr. Leachim is flexible. If the children do not understand something, they can repeat Mr. Leachim's lesson over and over again. When the children do a good job, he tells them something interesting about their hobbies. At the end of the lesson, the children switch off Mr. Leachim. The good thing about Mr. Leachim is that he doesn't have a nervous system like a human, so he doesn't get upset if a child is "difficult."

Today, scientists are trying to create a robot that shows emotions like a human being. At M.I.T. (Massachusetts Institute of Technology), Cynthia Breazeal has created a robot called Kismet. It has only a head at this time. As soon as Breazeal comes and sits in front of Kismet, the robot's

Notes
l. 1: smart = intelligent **brain** = an organ inside the head that controls movement, thought, memory, and feeling **l. 7: deliver** = take and hand over things to the proper person or place **l. 12: advantage** = a quality of something that makes it better or more useful **l. 16: enter** = push buttons to give a word or number **l. 19: flexible** = able to change easily **l. 22-23: switch off** = stop something electric by pushing a button or moving a bar **l. 24: nervous system** = the system of all the nerves in the body **l. 25: create** = bring into existence **emotion** = a strong human feeling

mood changes. The robot smiles. Breazeal talks to it the way a mother talks to a child, and Kismet watches and smiles. When Breazeal starts to move backward and forward, Kismet doesn't like that and looks upset. The message Kismet is giving is "Stop this!" Breazeal stops, and Kismet becomes calm. When Breazeal now pays no attention to Kismet, the robot becomes sad. When Breazeal turns toward Kismet, the robot is happy again. Another thing Kismet does like a child is to play with a toy and then become bored with the toy and close its eyes and go to sleep. Breazeal is still developing Kismet. Kismet still has many things missing in its personality. It does not have all human emotions yet, but one day it will!

At one time, people said that computers could not have emotions. It looks very possible that in the future scientists will develop a computer that does have emotions and can even be a friend. But what are the advantages of having a friend that's a machine?

(525 words)

Notes
l. 29: **mood** = the general way you feel   l. 33: **pay attention** = look and listen carefully

ocabulary

Complete the sentences with the following words.

| enters | pay attention | create | mood | flexible | switch off |
| emotions | smart |

1. Robots with their computer brains are _____.
2. Cynthia Breazeal is trying to _____ a robot that has feelings.
3. Kismet does not have _____ like love.
4. When a person looks at Kismet, the robot's _____ changes.
5. Kismet doesn't like it when you don't _____.
6. A child goes to Mr. Leachim and _____ an identification number.
7. When a child needs more time or needs Mr. Leachim to repeat something, the robot is _____.
8. When the lesson finishes, the child can _____ Mr. Leachim.

Looking for the Main Ideas

Circle the letter of the best answer.

1. Robots ____.
    a. can help people in regular jobs
    b. cannot help people do difficult jobs
    c. work only in hospitals
    d. work only in post offices
2. Mr. Leachim is a ____.
    a. mail carrier robot
    b. fourth-grade teacher
    c. fourth-grade teacher robot
    d. Help Mate robot
3. Kismet is a ____.
    a. dog robot
    b. robot that has some emotions
    c. robot that is just like a human
    d. Help Mate robot

Looking for Details

Circle T if the sentence is true. Circle F if the sentence is false.

(T F) 1. Bobby is a mail carrier robot in an office building.
(T F) 2. Hospitals use robots called Help Mates.
(T F) 3. Mr. Leachim identifies a child by his or her voice only.
(T F) 4. When the lesson is over, the child enters an identification number.
(T F) 5. Kismet cries when it doesn't like something.
(T F) 6. Kismet goes to sleep when it is bored.

iscussion

Discuss these questions with your classmates.

1. Discuss what you want robots to do in the future.

    _____

2. List four advantages (good things) and four disadvantages (bad things) of having a robot teacher.

    _____

    _____

    _____

    _____

Unit 2 The Shape of the Face

「自然エネルギー推進会議」の設立総会であいさつする小泉純一郎氏

小泉進次郎氏、東京都港区の復興庁にて

✓ Pre-Reading Activity

Discuss these questions.

1. How similar are the faces of the two people in the photos?

2. What is the shape of their faces?

3. Whom do you most look like in your family?

Reading

　　　　Some people believe that the shape of a person's face shows the general character of the person. The Chinese believe that there are eight basic shapes of the face, and each shape shows a special character. The shapes are round, diamond, rectangle, square, triangle, narrow forehead and
5　wide jaw, wide forehead and square chin, and wide forehead and high cheekbones. Here is what people say about these shapes.
　　　　Round faces have high and flat cheekbones, flat ears, wide noses, and strong mouths with thin lips. People with round faces are very intelligent, and they prefer to work with their brain instead of their body. People with
10　round faces are confident and usually live a long life.
　　　　Many movie stars and famous women have diamond faces. The diamond face is narrow at the top and has a pointed chin. The Chinese believe that it is lucky if you meet a man or a woman with a diamond face before you go to an important meeting. People with this type of face are
15　generally lucky in love and in their jobs. They may not be happy when they are young, but they get what they want later in their lives. People with diamond faces are warm, but they have a strong will.

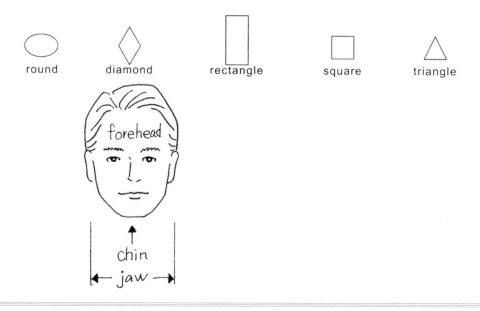

[Notes]

round, diamond, rectangle, square, triangle, forehead, chin, jaw = cf. the above illustrations　**l. 5: jaw** = the bony parts of the face that hold the teeth　**l. 6: cheekbones** = the bones below and beside the eyes　**l. 10: confident** = having a strong belief in your ability　**l. 17: will** = strength of mind to control your actions

People with rectangular faces control their feelings, but they are intelligent and creative. These people work hard and are very reliable. Their work is very important to them and comes before everything else, even family. They are not easy to be around when they do not feel free or when they feel bored. Many people with rectangular faces are at their best when they are older.

Square faces usually belong to men, but women can also have them. Men with this kind of face are good at making decisions and keeping to them. They are generous and honest. They put their friends first in everything. Both men and women with square faces are lucky and live a long life.

A wide forehead, high cheekbones, and a pointed chin make a triangular face. People with triangular faces are lively and intelligent and often stand out from others; however, they worry too much, and their emotions are fragile, so they can get depressed easily. Because of this, they do better in jobs where they work with people.

The Chinese believe that a person with a wide jaw and narrow forehead is like the earth and changes little. People with this kind of face love success and will almost always get what they want, especially money and all that it brings. A man with this kind of face will not be close to his children, but his children will respect his strength. A woman with this kind of face was Jacqueline Kennedy, who had a strong character even in difficult times.

People with wide foreheads and square chins are intelligent and work hard to get what they want. They can be calm and quiet, or they can be the opposite, too, because they like to get attention. Famous movie people like Leonardo DiCaprio and Angelina Jolie have this kind of face; so did Picasso, the painter. They usually have a long life and save their energy for important times in life.

People with wide foreheads and high cheekbones show strong character and a lot of energy. This helps them to be normal again if something bad happens. They know what they like and don't like to change their habits. Nevertheless, they like to live a full life.

(584 words)

Notes
l. 19: creative = showing artistic ability   **l. 26: generous** = willing to give   **l. 31: fragile** = easily broken

Vocabulary

Complete the sentences with the following words.

> will   confident   fragile   generous   creative   cheekbones   jaw

1. Some people have a wide _____, which makes their face look wide.
2. Women with high _____ look attractive.
3. People with a strong _____ are able to do what they have to do.
4. Artists are _____ people.
5. People with _____ emotions can get hurt very easily.
6. People with square faces are _____ with their time and money.
7. People with round faces are _____ and walk with their heads held up high.

Looking for the Main Ideas

Circle the letter of the best answer.

1. The Chinese believe that the shape of the face ____.
   a. is not important
   b. can show the character of a person
   c. is important when you want to be a movie star
   d. can show that a person has medical problems

2. The Chinese believe that there are ____.
   a. eight basic shapes of faces
   b. square faces and round faces only
   c. some good shapes and some bad shapes
   d. four basic shapes of faces

3. The Chinese believe that the shape of your face can show ____.
   a. when accidents will happen to you
   b. if you are intelligent
   c. if you are Chinese
   d. if you will have children

Looking for Details

(T F) 1. The Chinese believe that it is lucky to meet a person with a diamond face before an important meeting.

(T F) 2. Jacqueline Kennedy had a square face.

(T F) 3. The Chinese believe that round faces are intelligent.

(T F) 4. Angelina Jolie has a rectangular face.

(T F) 5. The Chinese believe that people with triangular faces can get depressed easily.

(T F) 6. The Chinese believe that people with diamond faces are not lucky in love.

Discussion

Discuss these questions with your classmates.

1. Do you think there is any truth in reading people's faces (physiognomy)? How reliable is it?

   _____

2. Discuss what shapes of face, eyes, mouth, ears, etc., show good character.

   _____

Unit 3: Killer Bees

✓ Pre-Reading Activity

Discuss these questions.

1. How are bees useful to people?

   _____

2. Are you afraid of bees? Why or why not?

   _____

Reading

Killer bees started in Brazil in 1957. A scientist in Sao Paulo wanted bees to make more honey, so he put forty-six African bees in with some Brazilian bees. The bees started to breed and make a new kind of bee. However, the new bees were a mistake. They did not want to make more honey; they wanted to attack. Then, by accident, twenty-six African bees escaped and bred with the Brazilian bees outside.

Scientists could not control the problem. The bees spread. They went from Brazil to Venezuela and then to Central America. Now they are in North America. They travel about 390 miles a year. Each group of bees, or colony, grows to four times its old size in a year. This means that there will be one million new colonies in five years.

Killer bees are very dangerous, and people are right to be afraid of them. When killer bees attack people, they attack in great numbers and often seriously hurt or kill people. Four hundred bee stings can kill a person. A total of 8,000 bee stings is not unusual for a killer bee attack. In fact, a student in Costa Rica had 10,000 stings and died. Often, the bees attack for no reason. They may attack because of a strong smell that is good or bad or because a person is wearing a dark color, has dark hair, or is wearing some kind of shiny jewelry.

What can you do if you see killer bees coming toward you? The first thing you can do is run——as fast as you can. Killer bees do not move very fast, but they will follow you up to one mile. Then you must go into the nearest house or tent. Do not jump into water. The bees will wait for you to come out of the water. Killer bees will try to attack the head or the face, so cover your head with a handkerchief or a coat. You may even take off your shirt and cover your head. Stings to your chest and back are not as dangerous as stings to your head and face. However, if the bees sting you many times, you must get medical attention immediately.

Notes

l. 3: **breed** = produce young   l. 5: **attack** = move toward violently   l. 6: **escape** = get away   l. 7: **spread** = cover a larger area   l. 10: **colony** = a community of animals of one kind living close together   l. 19: **shiny** = bright, filled with light   l. 27: **sting** = attack people or animals using the needle-like organ of an insect usually covered with poison   l. 28: **medical** = relating to practice of medicine

How are killer bees different from normal honey bees? Killer bees are a little smaller than regular bees, but only an expert can tell the difference. Killer bees get angry more easily and attack more often than honey bees. Killer bees attack and sting in great numbers. Like honey bees, each killer bee can sting only one time, and the female bee dies after it stings. Killer bees also make honey, but a honey bee makes five times more honey than a killer bee.

Up to now, killer bees have killed about 1,000 people and over 100,000 cows in the Americas. In the United States alone, five people have died from killer bee stings since 1990. The first American died from bee stings in Texas in 1993. From Texas, the bees moved to Nevada, New Mexico, Arizona, and then Southern California. Where will they go next?

(519 words)

Notes
l. 30: **expert** = a specialist, a person who is very skilful in a field l. 30: **tell the difference** = know one thing from another

Vocabulary

Complete the sentences with the following words.

> breed   attack   escaped   shiny   spread   tell the difference

1. It is not easy to _____ between a honey bee and a killer bee because they look almost the same.
2. Killer bees _____ people and animals for no reason.
3. Twenty-six African bees _____ outside.
4. The African bees and the Brazilian bees started to _____ and make a new kind of bee.
5. The new bees went from one country to another. They _____ quickly.
6. Killer bees attack people who are wearing _____ objects like jewelry.

Looking for the Main Ideas

Circle the letter of the best answer.

1. A scientist wanted bees ____.
   a. to go to Africa
   b. to make more honey
   c. to attack
   d. to breed more

2. Scientists ____.
   a. could not control the problem
   b. went to Brazil
   c. grew every year
   d. traveled to North America

3. People are afraid of killer bees because they ____.
   a. make honey
   b. attack and sting in large groups
   c. attack and die
   d. follow you

Looking for Details

Answer the questions with complete sentences.

1. Where did the killer bees go after they left Central America?

2. What colors do killer bees like to attack?

3. What part of the body do killer bees try to attack?

4. How many times does each killer bee sting?

5. When did the first American die from killer bees?

6. How many people have died from killer bees up to now?

Discussion

Discuss these questions with your classmates.

1. Have you been stung by a bee? What happened?

2. What is a good thing to do when a bee stings you?

3. What insects do you have in your country? Are these insects a problem?

4. What other insects or animals are you afraid of?

Unit 4 Celebrating Fifteen

✓ Pre-Reading Activity

Discuss these questions.

1. What is the girl in the photo wearing? Why?

   _____

2. What is a special day for a young person in your country? What does it mean?

   _____

3. How do people usually celebrate it?

   _____

Reading

A *quincenera* (pronounced "Kin-sin-year") is a special celebration held for many girls in Spanish-speaking communities of the United States and in Latin America on their fifteenth birthday. The celebration may be different in different countries. The word *quincenera* can refer to the celebration or to the girl. This birthday is special because it celebrates that a girl is not a child anymore and has become a woman. It is a very important day for many young girls, a day they dream about for a long time. Everyone who knows the girl will celebrate it with a church ceremony and a big party.

There is a lot of preparation before a *quincenera* celebration. The most important and expensive thing is the girl's dress. The dress is like a bride's dress but is usually pink; however, today many girls wear dresses in other light colors, also. The birthday girl chooses fourteen girls and fourteen boys who will be her attendants at the ceremony and the dinner dance that follows. Traditionally, these girls and boys are younger than the birthday girl, but sometimes they are the same age. The dresses for the girls must be in the same color and style, just as the suits for the boys are in the same color and style. The reason for this is that all eyes will go to the birthday girl on that special day. Then the family orders a cake that is special like a wedding cake. Sometimes the godparents pay for it. Many times, the cake is so big that it needs a special table. Next, the parents rent a hall for the party and rent a band to play music. After that, they decide on the special food to serve the guests. Often a *quincenera* celebration can cost as much as a big wedding; the size of the party depends on how much the girl's parents can afford.

On the night before the girl's fifteenth birthday, a band plays in the evening outside her window. Then the day of her birthday arrives. First, the girl's family, her godparents, and her attendants go to a religious ceremony in the church. The girl receives a bouquet of flowers and blessings and prayers that will help her to live a strong life. Her parents are proud of their grown-up daughter, and they embrace her. Then she leaves the church with

Notes

l. 4: refer to = mean   **l. 13: attendant** = a person whose job is to serve or help people in a public place   **l. 19: godparent** = an adult who is a close family friend and guides you through your life   **l. 23: afford** = have enough money for   **l. 26: religious**>religion, the belief in the existence of a god or gods   **l. 27: bouquet** = a bunch of flowers   **blessing** = ask for God's help and protection for someone or something   **l. 28: proud of** = pleased because of something the person has done   **l. 29: embrace** = hug

her attendants and goes to the hall for the special party. Before they go to the party, they pose for photographs.

The hall is beautifully decorated with flowers, and it is full of guests. They wait for the girl and her family to arrive. The band plays music, and the party begins with a dinner. After the dinner, the girl dances the first dance with her father. Then the other attendants start to dance, followed by the guests. Everyone has a good time, and they all dance until midnight. It is a day she will always remember.

(492 words)

Notes
l. 31: **pose** = hold yourself still for a photograph

Vocabulary

Complete the sentences with the following words.

> attendants   afford   godparents   proud of   pose   blessings

1. A *quincenera* is expensive, and many parents cannot _____ to have one for their daughter.
2. The girl's _____ help her with guidance and advice throughout her life.
3. The *quincenera* chooses a total of twenty-eight _____.
4. In the church, the girl receives prayers and _____.
5. When the ceremony ends, the parents are _____ their daughter.
6. The *quincenera* and her attendants _____ for photos with which to remember this special day.

Looking for the Main Ideas

Circle the letter of the best answer.

1. A *quincenera* is ____.
    a. another name for a big birthday party
    b. a fifteenth birthday celebration held for girls in many Latin American countries
    c. the word for "woman" in Spanish
    d. a special birthday for boys and girls when they are fifteen
2. Before the *quincenera*, ____.
    a. the girl must make a dress
    b. there is a lot of preparation
    c. the girl asks fourteen boys to dance with her
    d. the girl's parents make a cake
3. On the day of the *quincenera*, there is ____.
    a. only a church ceremony
    b. a church ceremony, a dinner, and a dance
    c. only a dinner and a dance
    d. a party for the girl's relatives

Looking for Details

Use complete sentences to answer the questions.

1. What is the traditional color for the *quincenera*'s dress?

2. How many girl and boy attendants does she have?

3. What do her parents rent?

4. What does the girl receive at the religious ceremony?

5. Where does she go with her attendants after the church ceremony?

6. With whom does the *quincenera* dance first?

Discussion

Discuss these questions with your classmates.

1. How do people celebrate a special day for children in your country?

2. Describe a wedding in your country.

Unit 5: A Folktale

✓ Pre-Reading Activity

Discuss these questions.

1. Do you know any famous folktales?

2. Why do people like them?

3. What is your favorite folktale?

Reading

This story happened a long time ago, somewhere in Europe, in the middle of a bitter winter. There was a terrible famine throughout the land. In the villages, people were so hungry that each family kept their food hidden away, so that no one else would be able to find it. They hardly spoke to each other, and if any food was found, they fought over it.

One day, a poor traveler arrived in a village and set up his tent by the side of the road. He had with him a large pot, a wooden spoon, and a stone. "You can't stay here," said the villagers. "There's no food for you!" And they raced back to their houses to make sure no one would steal their food while they were away. "That doesn't matter," said the stranger. "I have everything I need."

He gathered sticks and built a fire in the middle of the main square. Then he placed his pot on the fire and added some water. He glanced around and noticed that he was being watched from every window and from every doorway. He smiled with satisfaction as the steam rose from the pot. Next, he took an ordinary stone from his pocket, which he carefully placed in the pot. He stirred the soup and waited patiently for it to boil.

By this time, the villagers were full of curiosity. Several of them had gathered around the pot. "What are you making?" they asked. "Stone soup," replied the man. "It smells good, doesn't it?" And he sniffed the soup and smiled in anticipation. "Of course, a little salt and pepper would really help the flavor." "I think I could find some salt and pepper," said one of the women, and she ran back to her house to fetch the salt and pepper to add to the soup. "How tasty it would be with a tiny piece of garlic," said the traveler. "I might have a tiny piece of garlic," said another villager. "If only we had some potatoes, too, then it would really be delicious," said the stranger. "I'll get you a potato," said another man and rushed home to fetch it.

Soon the rumor had spread around the whole village. Someone was

> [Notes]
>
> l. 2: **famine** = a time when many people have no food   l. 6: **tent** = temporary shelter that a person can carry   l. 13: **glance** = look at something briefly   l. 15: **steam** = what rises into the air when water gets very hot   l. 18: **curiosity** = desire to find out more about something   l. 29: **rumor** = news that may or may not be true

30 making a delicious soup with a special stone. People came from every house to smell the bubbling soup, and each of them brought an extra ingredient to make the soup taste even better. They were so hungry, and the soup smelled so good. "It must be that special stone," they said.

Finally, the man declared that the soup was ready and it was time to
35 eat. The villagers each brought a dish, and there was plenty of food for everyone. They talked and laughed, and for a while they forgot the famine and the cold. Even long after the famine had ended, people still remembered that night and the finest soup they had ever tasted. (491 words)

Vocabulary

Complete the sentences with the following words.

> famine   tent   rumor   glanced   curiosity   steam

1. A _____ is a shelter that you can fold up and carry with you.
2. The news may be true, or it may just be a _____.
3. When there is no food in a country, there is a _____.
4. They asked a lot of questions because they could not control their _____.
5. He _____ at the book, but didn't look at it carefully.
6. When you boil water, you can see _____.

Understanding the Story

Write complete answers to these questions.

1. What was happening in the villages of the land?

2. Why were the villagers hiding their food?

3. Why were they unfriendly to the traveler?

4. Why were they curious about the stone soup?

5. What kind of man was the traveler?

6. How did he make the villagers share their food?

7. What was the traveler's trick?

8. Why would the villagers never forget the stone soup?

_____

Interpreting the Story

Circle the letter of the best answer.

1. In the story, the villagers represent _____.
    a. people who think only of themselves
    b. people who work together
    c. people who are generous
    d. people who like to cook

2. In the story, the traveler represents _____.
    a. someone who helps people to work in a team
    b. someone who forces people to like each other
    c. someone who gives help when it is needed
    d. someone who prefers to be alone

3. In the story, the soup represents _____.
    a. something everyone wants but can't have
    b. something everyone can make individually
    c. something everyone can make together
    d. something everyone hates

4. What is the moral (the lesson) of the story?
    a. Everyone can be successful if he or she wants.
    b. No one is better than anyone else.
    c. People can achieve more by helping each other.
    d. Think before you act.

Discussion

Discuss these questions with your classmates.

1. How did you learn about folktales in your culture?

   _____

2. Are folktales less important today than they were in the past? Why?

   _____

3. What can we learn from folktales, and how useful are they in our daily lives?

   _____

Unit 6 Lightning

✓ Pre-Reading Activity

Discuss these questions.

1. What is happening in the picture?

2. How can lightning be dangerous?

3. What can you do to protect against a lightning strike?

Reading

Every second of every day, all over the world, there are more than 100 lightning bolts. That's about ten million lightning bolts in one day! Lightning amazes us, but it can also frighten us. We have good reason to be afraid of lightning. Every year, about 100 people in the United States and Canada die from lightning, and another 300 are injured. It is strange that of all the people who die from lightning, 84 percent are men. Lightning is the main cause of forest fires; it starts more than 9,000 fires each year.

Lightning is electricity inside a cloud. Scientists do not know exactly what makes this electricity. But they know that the electricity inside a cloud can be as much as 100 million volts. From this extremely strong electricity, a lightning bolt, like a streak of bright light, comes down from the sky. Its temperature can reach 50,000 degrees Fahrenheit within a few millionths of a second. That's almost five times the temperature on the sun's surface. The lightning bolt is very quick. It can move at a speed of 87,000 miles per second. A rocket traveling at this speed would reach the moon in 2.5 seconds. With the lightning bolt, we usually hear thunder, which is the sound of hot air exploding. Lightning and thunder happen at exactly the same time, but we see lightning first because light travels a million times faster than sound.

Lightning often strikes tall buildings. However, many buildings have lightning rods to protect them from lightning. When lightning strikes, the electricity goes safely down the metal rod to the ground. Benjamin Franklin, the American statesman, invented the lightning rod in 1760. That is why buildings like the Empire State Building in New York City are safe. Lightning may hit this building as many as twelve times in twenty minutes and as often as 500 times a year. Airplanes are not as easy to protect as buildings, and accidents do happen. In 1963, a Boeing 707 jet was hit by lightning and crashed. 81 people died.

If you see thunder and lightning coming, here are some things you can do to protect yourself. Go inside a house, get into a car, or go under a

---

Notes

l. 2: **lightning bolt** = bright flash of light you see in the sky during a storm   l. 3: **amaze** = surprise greatly   **frighten** = make afraid   l. 5: **injure** = hurt   l. 12: **temperature** = the degree or intensity of heat   l. 16: **explode** = blow apart, like a bomb   l. 20: **rod** = a thin, straight stick made of wood or metal   **protect** = stop someone or something from being harmed   l. 22: **statesman** = a politician   l. 26: **crash** = (of an aircraft) fall from the sky and hit the ground or sea

bridge. If you cannot find shelter, go to the lowest point on the ground. If you are outside, remember that trees attract lightning, especially tall trees. Never go under a tall tree that stands alone. If you are in a field, drop to your knees, bend forward, and put your hands on your knees. Do not lie down because the wet ground can carry lightning. Stay away from a lake, an ocean, or any other water. Don't touch or go near anything metal, such as a metal fence, golf clubs, and bicycles, because metal attracts lightning very quickly. Don't use a telephone except in an emergency.

They say that lightning never hits the same place twice, but this is not true. One man, Roy Sullivan, was hit by lightning seven different times in his life. He was injured each time but did not die. He died in 1983, but not from lightning. He killed himself because he loved a woman, but she didn't love him!

(537 words)

Notes
l. 30: shelter = building or place where you are safe from harm   **l. 31: attract** = make someone or something want to come there   **l. 37: emergency** = a serious, unexpected, and often dangerous situation

Vocabulary

Complete the sentences with the following words.

> frightened   injured   protects   shelter   attract   lightning bolts
> amaze   exploding

1. There are millions of _____ every day.
2. A sky with lightning can _____ you.
3. Many people are _____ when they see lightning because it is dangerous.
4. When lightning strikes people, they can be _____ or die.
5. Thunder sounds as if fireworks are _____.
6. A lightning rod _____ buildings from lightning strikes.
7. In a storm, you should find _____ from the bad weather.
8. Tall buildings _____ lightning strikes.

Looking for the Main Ideas

Circle the letter of the best answer.

1. Lightning ____.
    a. is not dangerous
    b. kills only men
    c. kills and injures many people
    d. happens about 100 times a day

2. Lightning ____.
    a. and thunder happen at the same time
    b. is as hot as the surface of the sun
    c. comes after thunder
    d. is hot air exploding

3. Lightning often strikes ____.
    a. Americans
    b. tall men
    c. tall buildings
    d. New York City

Looking for Details

Use complete sentences to answer the questions.

1. How many people die from lightning in the United States and Canada every year?

2. Why do we see lightning before we hear thunder?

3. Why is it not a good idea to touch metal when there's lightning?

4. Which building in New York City gets hit by lightning 500 times a year?

5. Who invented the lightning rod?

6. How did Roy Sullivan die?

Discussion

Discuss these questions with your classmates.

1. Why do you think more men than women die from lightning?

2. The disasters that we are most likely to remember are those that happen closest to where we live. Can you remember a disaster (fire, earthquake, etc.) that happened near where you live? Describe it.

Unit 7 Potatoes

✓ Pre-Reading Activity

Discuss these questions.

1. How often do you eat potatoes?

   _____

2. What do you eat French fries with?

   _____

3. How do you like to eat your potatoes?

   _____

Reading

Can you imagine life without French fries? Potatoes are very popular today. They are the fourth most important crop in the world, after wheat, rice, and corn. But in the past, potatoes were not always popular. People in Europe started to eat them only 200 years ago!

In the 1500s, the Spanish went to South America to look for gold. There, they found people eating potatoes. The people of Peru in South America had been eating potatoes for 7,000 years! The Spanish brought the potato back to Europe with them. But people in Europe did not like this strange vegetable. Some people thought that if you ate potatoes, your skin would look like the skin of a potato. Other people could not believe that you ate the underground part of the plant, so they ate the leaves instead. This made them sick because there is poison in the leaves. Others grew potatoes for their flowers. At one time in France, potato flowers were one of the most expensive flowers. Marie Antoinette, the wife of King Louis XVI, wore potato flowers in her hair.

Around 1780, the people of Ireland started to eat potatoes. They found that potatoes had many advantages. The potato grew on poor land, and it grew well in their cold and rainy climate. It gave more food than any other plant, and it needed little work. All they had to do was to plant the potatoes, and then they could do other work on the farm. On a small piece of land, a farmer could grow enough potatoes to feed his family. A person could eat 8 to 10 pounds of potatoes a day, with some milk or cheese, and be very healthy. Soon, potatoes became the main food in Ireland. Then, in 1845, a disease killed all the potatoes in Ireland. Two million people died of hunger. Many Irish who did not die came to the United States at this time. Over a million Irish came to America; one of them was the great-grandfather of John F. Kennedy.

In other parts of Europe, people did not want to change their old food habits. Some preferred to die of hunger rather than eat potatoes. In 1774, King Frederick of Germany wanted to stop his people from dying of

Notes

l. 1: **imagine** = have a picture in your mind about something   l. 11: **instead** = in place of   l. 12: **poison** = something that can kill you if you eat or drink it   l. 17: **advantage** = something that makes it helpful or useful   l. 22: **one pound** = 0.454 kilogram   l. 24: **disease** = a sickness   l. 26: **great-grandfather** = the father of the grandfather

hunger. He understood that potatoes were a good food, so he told the people to plant and eat potatoes or else his men would cut off their noses. The people were not happy, but they had no choice and so started to eat potatoes. Today, people in this part of Germany eat more potatoes than any other nationality. Each person eats about 370 pounds of potatoes every year!

Today, many countries have their own potato dishes. Germans eat potato salad, and the United States has the baked potato. And, of course, the French invented French fries. Now French fries are popular all over the world. The English eat them with salt and vinegar, the French eat them with salt and pepper, the Belgians eat them with mayonnaise, and the Americans eat them with ketchup.

(515 words)

Notes
l. 35: nationality = a group of people with the same language, culture and history in a nation state   **l. 36: dish** = special cooked food of some kind   **l. 37: baked** = cooked in the oven   **l. 38: invent** = think of or make for the first time   **l. 39: vinegar** = a sharp-tasting and sour liquid used for salad, sushi, pickles, etc.

Vocabulary

Complete the sentences with the following words.

> dishes   invented   poison   advantage   baked   instead
> imagine   disease

1. We cannot _____ eating a hamburger without French fries.
2. Some plants have _____ in them and can kill you if you eat them.
3. People didn't grow potatoes for food; they grew them for their flowers _____.
4. The potato got a _____, which killed the plants.
5. Americans cook the potato with its skin in the oven. They call it a _____ _____ potato.
6. From the name, we know that the French _____ French fries.
7. There are many _____ you can make with potatoes.
8. The potato has one big _____ over other crops—it is easy to grow.

Looking for the Main Ideas

Circle the letter of the best answer.

1. Potatoes are ____.
   a. popular today
   b. not popular today
   c. popular only in America
   d. popular only in Europe
2. In the 1500s, people in Europe ____.
   a. liked the potato
   b. had bad skin
   c. did not like the potato as food
   d. invented French fries

3. In about 1780, people started to ____.
   a. eat potatoes in Ireland
   b. grow potatoes for their flowers
   c. go to Peru
   d. die of hunger in America
4. French fries are ____.
   a. a special dish in Belgium
   b. popular all over the world
   c. from Germany
   d. most popular in America

Looking for Details

One word in each sentence is not correct. Rewrite the sentence with the correct word.

1. Potatoes grew in Europe 7,000 years ago.

   _____

2. In the 1700s, the Spanish brought the potato back to Europe.

   _____

3. There is poison in the skin of the potato.

   _____

4. A disease killed the people in Ireland in 1845.

   _____

5. Five million people died of hunger in Ireland.

   _____

6. The potato dish of Germany is the baked potato.

   _____

7. The Americans invented French fries.

   _____

Discussion

Discuss these questions with your classmates.

1. Find out from the students in your class about the main food and drink in their country. Fill out the questionnaire below.

Name	Country	Main Food	Main Drink
Berta	Mexico	Tortillas	Coffee

2. Is the main drink in your country good for you? Why or why not?

   _____

3. In your country, are there any customs related to the main food?

   _____

Unit 8
Right Brain or Left Brain?

✓ Pre-Reading Activity

Discuss these questions.

1. Do you know the names of the people in the picture above?

   _____

2. What are they famous for?

   _____

3. All of them are the same in one way. What do you think it is?

   _____

Reading

What do Leonardo da Vinci, Paul McCartney, and Julia Roberts have in common? They are all left-handed. Today about 15 percent of the population is left-handed. But why are people left-handed? The answer may be in the way the brain works.

Our brain is like a message center. Each second, the brain receives more than a million messages from our body and knows what to do with them. People think that the weight of the brain tells how intelligent you are, but this isn't true. Albert Einstein's brain weighed 1,375 grams, but less intelligent people have heavier brains. What is important is the quality of the brain. The brain has two halves— the right brain and the left brain. Each half is about the same size. The right half controls the left side of the body, and the left half controls the right side of the body. One half is usually stronger than the other. One half of the brain becomes stronger when you are a child and usually stays the stronger half for the rest of your life.

The left side of the brain controls the right side of the body, so when the left brain is stronger, the right hand will be strong and the person may be right-handed. The left half controls speaking, so a person with a strong left brain may become a good speaker, professor, lawyer, or salesperson. A person with a strong left brain may have a strong idea of time and will probably be punctual. The person may be strong in math and logic and may like to have things in order. He or she may remember people's names and like to plan things ahead. He or she may be practical and safe. If something happens to the left side of the brain, the person may have problems speaking and may not know what day it is. The right side of his or her body will become weak.

When the right side of the brain is stronger, the person will have a strong left hand and may be left-handed. The person may prefer art, music, and literature. The person may become an artist, a writer, an inventor, a film

Notes
l. 1-2: have something in common = have the same interests, ideas, etc.   **l. 3: population** = number of people who live in a place   **l. 5: message** = instruction or news sent to someone or something   **l. 7: weight** = how heavy something or someone is   **l. 8: weigh** = measure how heavy something/someone is   **l. 18: salesperson** = a person whose job is to sell goods   **l. 20: punctual** = on time, not late   **logic** = thinking that follows rules   **l. 21: have things in order** = have things in their right place   **l. 22: ahead** = earlier, in advance   **practical** = realistic   **l. 28: literature** = novels, plays, and poems   **l. 28-29: film director** = a person who is the leader in movie making and tells the actors and staff what to do

director, or a photographer. The person may recognize faces, but not
remember names. The person may not love numbers or business. The person may like to use his or her feelings and not look at logic and what is practical. If there is an accident to the right side of the brain, the person may not know where he or she is and may not be able to do simple hand movements.

This does not mean that all artists are left-handed and all accountants are right-handed. There are many exceptions. Some right-handers have a strong right brain, and some left-handers have a strong left brain. The best thing would be to use both right and left sides of the brain. There are people who learn to do two things at the same time. They can answer practical questions on the telephone (which uses the left brain) and at the same time play the piano (which uses the right brain), but this is not easy to do!

(532 words)

Notes
l. 29: recognize = remember having heard or seen before   **l. 34: accountant** = a person whose job is to keep and check a financial situation   **l. 35: exception** = people or things that do not belong with the others

Vocabulary

Complete the sentences with the following words.

> punctual   recognize   have things in order   exceptions   logic
> population   in common   message

1. Leonardo da Vinci and Julia Roberts have something _____. They are both left-handed.
2. About 15 percent of the _____ is left-handed.
3. Each part of our body sends a _____ to the brain.
4. Right-handed people may not do something because they feel like it. They may do it because there is _____ to it.
5. A right-handed person may like to be neat and _____.
6. A left-handed person may look at a face and _____ the person.
7. A right-handed person doesn't like to be late. He or she is _____.
8. We cannot say that all right-handers have strong left brains and all left-handers have strong right brains. There are _____.

Looking for the Main Ideas

Read the passage and look for the main ideas. Circle the letter of the best answer.

1. People are right-handed or left-handed because of ____.
   a. the population
   b. the way the brain works
   c. Paul McCartney and Julia Roberts
   d. the messages the brain receives

2. The brain ____.
   a. has two halves
   b. has two left halves
   c. is heavier in intelligent people
   d. is lighter in intelligent people

3. Each side of the brain ____.
   a. likes language and math
   b. controls the same things
   c. controls different things
   d. changes all the time

Looking for Details

Read the passage again and look for details. Circle T if the sentence is true. Circle F if the sentence is false.

(T F) 1. Fifty percent of the population is left-handed.

(T F) 2. The weight of the brain does not tell how intelligent you are.

(T F) 3. A right-handed person may prefer music and art.

(T F) 4. A person with a strong right brain may be good at remembering people's names.

(T F) 5. Some people can use both sides of the brain at the same time.

(T F) 6. A person with a strong right brain may not be practical.

Discussion

Discuss these questions with your classmates.

1. Do you think children should be forced to be right-handed?

2. Does the word left have a negative meaning in your language? Is it bad to be left-handed in your country?

3. Ask a left-handed person these questions:
   - Are your parents left-handed?
   - When you were a child, did people try to make you right-handed?
   - Do you want to be right-handed?
   - What things do you find difficult to use (for example, scissors, can openers)?

   In groups, discuss the answers you get.

Unit 9: Louis Braille

✓ Pre-Reading Activity

Discuss these questions.

1. What are the hands in the picture doing?

   _____

2. How can blind people read?

   _____

3. What do you know about blind people?

   _____

Reading

Louis Braille was born near Paris, France, in 1809. When he was a little boy, Louis loved to play with his father's tools. One day, when he was four, he was playing with his father's tools when a sharp tool went into his left eye. An infection started in his left eye and went to the other eye. He was unlucky. A few weeks later, Louis was blind.

When Louis was ten, his parents took him to a school for blind children in Paris. Louis lived at the school. He was a good student and looked forward to the day when he could read. The school had some books that blind people could read. These books had letters that stood out. He had to feel each letter with his fingers. There was one sentence on each page. Just one part of a book weighed 20 pounds. A whole book weighed 400 pounds! By age eleven, Louis had read all fourteen books in the school. He wanted to read more, but there were no more books. So every evening, he tried to find a way for blind people to be able to read books. One day, Captain Charles Barbier, a French soldier, came to speak at the school. Barbier had invented night-writing. This system used dots for the letters of the alphabet. Soldiers could feel the dots with their fingers and read with no light. Barbier thought night-writing could also help blind people.

Barbier's system was difficult, but it gave Louis an idea. He worked night after night to make a simple system with dots. By age fifteen, he had finished his system. He showed it to other students in the school, and they loved it. They called it Braille after him. At age seventeen, Louis graduated from the school and became a teacher there. In his free time, he copied books into Braille. Someone read to Louis while he made the dots. He copied the books of Shakespeare and other writers into Braille. The students read all the books and wanted more. The school did not want a fifteen-year-old boy's invention to be better than their own heavy books and would not let students read Braille books. Nevertheless, the students continued to read them.

Notes

l. 3: tool = something you use for doing work   **sharp** = able to cut easily   **l. 4: infection** = a disease you get from something or someone   **l. 5: unlucky** = having bad things happen by chance   **blind** = not able to see   **l. 8: look forward to** = wait with happiness for   **l. 9: letter** = a written symbol for a sound or an alphabet   **stand out** = is easily seen or recognized   **l. 16: night-writing** = a device with which you can see things with no light   **dot** = a small round point   **l. 24: copy** = make or do something that is the same as something else

Finally, after twenty years, the school agreed to use Braille.

Louis Braille spent the rest of his life trying to tell the world about Braille. But nobody cared. Louis was unlucky again. He became very sick. Even when he was sick in his bed, he continued to write books in Braille for the students at his school. A few years later, Louis Braille died at age forty-three. Two years after he died, schools for the blind began to use his system.

Today, we use Braille not only to write words in all languages, but also to write math and music. Blind people send Braille greeting cards, wear Braille watches, type on Braille keyboards, and take elevators with Braille controls. Louis Braille had no idea how many people he had helped. On the door of the house where he was born are the words "He opened the doors of knowledge to all those who cannot see."

(529 words)

Notes
l. 29: agree = say yes; give permission

Vocabulary

Complete the sentences with the following words.

> an infection   copied   dots   blind   sharp   unlucky
> tools   looked forward to

1. When Louis was a child, he played with his father's _____.
2. A _____ tool went into his eye.
3. Louis got _____ in his eye.
4. Louis became _____ when he was four years old.
5. Louis liked school and _____ the day when he could read.
6. Barbier's system used _____.
7. Louis was _____ again in life.
8. Louis _____ other books into Braille.

Looking for the Main Ideas

Circle the letter of the best answer.

1. When Louis was four, he ____.
    a. became blind
    b. had sharp tools
    c. went to school
    d. read books
2. Charles Barbier ____.
    a. had an infection
    b. invented night-writing
    c. visited soldiers
    d. became a teacher
3. By age fifteen, Louis ____.
    a. had died
    b. was difficult
    c. made a new system of reading
    d. had copied many books

Looking for Details

One word in each sentence is not correct. Rewrite the sentence with the correct word.

1. When Louis was four, a blind tool went into his eye.

2. Louis went to a school for unlucky children in Paris.

3. Barbier's system used tools for the letters of the alphabet.

4. Barbier thought his system could help blind people to play.

5. Louis died at age thirty-four.

6. Today, we use Braille not only to write words in all languages, but also to write art and music.

iscussion

Discuss these questions with your classmates.

1. Do you know of other famous blind people? How are blind people special?

   _____

2. Louis Braille was unlucky. Do you know another unlucky person? Explain.

   _____

Unit 10
Laws about Children

✔ Pre-Reading Activity

Discuss these questions.

1. Do you think these children are happy?

2. Do you think children can work in a factory in Japan today?

3. What laws do you know about work by children?

Reading

In general, laws about children are a good thing. One hundred years ago in industrial countries, children worked eighteen hours a day in a factory at age seven. The factory owner could beat a child who fell asleep or was not fast enough. Both parents and teachers could do whatever they liked to children because children had no protection under the law.

Today, there are many laws to protect children all over the world. Some people think that children must obey rules or be punished. Other people do not agree. The Inuit, or Eskimos, in Alaska almost never hit their children. If the children don't obey, the parents make fun of them.

Children in the United States are not as lucky as Inuit children. Parents can spank their children at home. Similarly, schools can punish children by spanking or hitting as long as it is "reasonable." There are rules about what is reasonable. These rules look at the child's age, the child's past behavior, why the person is hitting the child, and so on. However, the law says that officials cannot hit people in prisons or mental hospitals in the United States. Some people think it is not fair that officials can hit schoolchildren and not prisoners. Many school districts have their own laws and rules that forbid hitting students. These laws change from state to state. It really depends on where you live in the United States. In contrast, in Sweden, it is against the law for anyone——parent or teacher——to hit a child.

In the United States, all children must go to school until the age of sixteen. However, in some states, like Hawaii, Utah, and Washington, children must attend school until the age of eighteen! A child cannot miss school without an acceptable excuse. There are laws about this. Illness, a death in the family, or an emergency is an acceptable excuse for missing a class or a whole day. Schools are very serious about school attendance. There are laws that make the parents accountable if their children miss school. Parents can go to jail or pay a fine. In Colorado, a fifteen-year-old girl went to jail for a month because she missed forty-three days of school and was late nineteen times. Her parents also went to jail for ten days and paid a fine of $300.

Notes

l. 3: **beat** = hit again and again   l. 7: **punish** = make someone feel pain for doing something wrong   l. 9: **make fun of** = laugh at   l. 16: **fair** = correct and right   l. 18: **forbid** = do not allow; make it against the rules
l. 24: **excuse** = reason   l. 28: **pay a fine** = pay money for doing something wrong

In the United States, all children must attend school, and they have the right to do this for free. All children have the right to go to school; it does not matter what their race, sex, or religion is, whether they are American citizens or illegal residents who speak no English, or whether they are disabled in any way. Children can leave school when they are sixteen, whether or not they graduate, and can continue their education until they are twenty-one or they graduate from high school, whichever comes first. However, children do not have the right to attend any school they choose. The law says they must attend school in the community where they live.

The law says children are adults at age eighteen. In the United States, they can work or live away from home and be independent. However, if they want to work before the age of eighteen and are still students, they must not work during school hours. They can work only three hours a day when there is school and not more than forty hours a week when there is no school.

(580 words)

Notes
l. 41: independent = free, not controlled

Vocabulary

Complete the sentences with the following words.

> make fun of   be punished   forbid   pay a fine   beat
> fair   excuse   independent

1. The Inuit almost never _____ their children.
2. When the children do not obey, Inuit parents _____ their children.
3. Many states have laws that _____ hitting students.
4. If you are sick and have a letter from a doctor, it is a good _____ to miss a day of school.
5. Sometimes, parents _____ or go to jail if they let their children miss school.
6. In the old days, children used to _____ for no good reason.
7. The laws let officials hit schoolchildren and not prisoners. Some people think this is not _____.
8. After the age of eighteen, if a person works, lives away from home, and pays for himself or herself, that person is _____.

Looking for the Main Ideas

Circle the letter of the best answer.

1. Laws about children are ____.
   a. not a good idea
   b. only for parents
   c. a good thing
   d. for Americans only
2. In the United States, ____.
   a. parents cannot hit children
   b. parents can hit children
   c. school officials cannot hit children
   d. parents and teachers cannot hit children

3. In the United States, all children must ____.

   a. go to school at least until age eighteen

   b. pay to go to school

   c. graduate from high school

   d. go to school at least until age sixteen

Looking for Details

Circle T if the sentence is true. Circle F if the sentence is false.

(T F) 1. Children must attend school until age eighteen in Hawaii.

(T F) 2. Illegal residents in the United States cannot get a free education.

(T F) 3. In Sweden, parents and teachers cannot hit children.

(T F) 4. In the United States, a person is an adult at age sixteen.

(T F) 5. In the United States, you don't have the right to go to any school you choose.

(T F) 6. Parents can go to jail if their children miss a lot of school.

Discussion

Discuss these questions with your classmates.

1. Discuss whether it is good or bad for a parent to hit a child.

2. Do you think that teachers in schools should have the right to hit a child?

3. Many young people want to be independent as soon as they can. What are some responsibilities of being independent?

Unit 11: The World's Most Unusual Millionaire

✓ Pre-Reading Activity

Discuss these questions.

1. Who are some famous millionaires today?

   _____

2. What kinds of things do they own?

   _____

3. Imagine you are a millionaire. What will you spend your money on? Check the boxes, and discuss your answers.

   ☐ expensive car   ☐ beautiful home   ☐ other

   ☐ expensive clothes   ☐ nice vacations

Reading

Hetty Robinson was born in 1834. When her parents died, she was thirty years old. They left her $10 million ($185 million in today's dollars). She was very good at business and soon made more money. Hetty was famous as the richest woman in the United States, but she was also famous because she was very stingy.

Even when she was young, she was stingy. For instance, on her twenty-first birthday, she refused to light the candles on her birthday cake because she did not want to waste them. The next day, she cleaned the candles and returned them to the store to get a refund.

Hetty always thought men wanted to marry her for her money. Finally, at the age of thirty-three, she decided to get married because she did not want her relatives to get her money. She married Edward Green, who was a millionaire. They had a son and a daughter. Soon after, Hetty divorced him because she did not agree with him about money matters.

Hetty was even stingy with her own child. For example, when her son hurt his knee in an accident, Hetty did not call a doctor. She tried to take care of it herself. When her son's knee didn't get better, she dressed him in old clothes and took him to a free clinic. The doctors recognized her and asked for money. Hetty refused to pay and took her son home. The boy did not get medical treatment, and a few years later his leg was amputated.

Hetty was stingy with herself, too. For example, she always wore the same black dress. As the years passed by, the color of the dress changed from black to green and then brown. When the dress became dirty, she went to a cheap laundry and told them to wash only the bottom where it was dirty, and she waited until it was ready. Her undergarments were old newspapers she got from the streets. She rented a cheap apartment with no heat in New Jersey because she did not want to pay taxes in New York. Then she traveled on the train to her office in New York. Her office was a space in

Notes

l. 5: **stingy** = not wanting to spend or give away money   l. 7: **refuse** = say that you will not do or take something   l. 8: **waste** = not use; use when it is not necessary   l. 9: **refund** = money you get back for something you bought   l. 13: **millionaire** = a person who has one million dollars or pounds, a very rich person   **divorce** = legally end a marriage   l. 18: **clinic** = a building where people can go for medical treatment   l. 20: **medical treatment** = care given by doctors   **amputate** = cut off by surgical operation   l. 24: **laundry** = a store where they wash and iron clothes   l. 25: **undergarment** = underclothing, underwear   l. 28: **space** = empty area

a bank, which the bank gave to her for free. All she ate was raw onions and cold oatmeal. She was too stingy to spend money to heat her food. Sometimes, to heat her oatmeal, she put it on the office heater because that was free. She also ate cookies, but regular cookies were too expensive for her, so she walked a long way to get broken cookies, which were much cheaper. One time, she spent half the night looking for a two-cent stamp.

When Hetty Green died in 1916, she had no friends. She left more than $100 million (over $17 billion today) to her son and daughter. Her son and daughter were not stingy like Hetty, and they spent the money freely.

(492 words)

Notes
l. 29: **raw** = not cooked

ocabulary

Complete the sentences with the following words.

> waste   medical treatment   laundry   space   refund   stingy
> raw   refused

1. Hetty did not like to spend money; she was _____.
2. Hetty went to the _____ to have the bottom part of her dress washed.
3. On her twenty-first birthday, Hetty _____ to light the candles on her cake.
4. Hetty liked to use everything. She did not like to _____ anything.
5. She went back to the store to get a _____ of the money she paid for the birthday candles.
6. Her son hurt his knee, but he did not get _____.
7. The bank gave Hetty a _____ to use as her office.
8. Hetty did not cook onions; she ate them _____.

Looking for the Main Ideas

Circle the letter of the best answer.

1. Hetty was a very rich woman, but she was _____.
   a. stingy
   b. short
   c. green
   d. old

2. Hetty married _____.
   a. for love
   b. to have children
   c. so that her relatives would not get her money
   d. so that she would not be lonely

3. Hetty was even stingy with _____.
   a. Edward Green
   b. her own child
   c. her leg
   d. her parents

Looking for Details

Circle T if the answer is true. Circle F if the answer is false.

(T F) 1. Hetty's parents died when she was thirty.
(T F) 2. Hetty ate mostly raw onions and cold oatmeal.
(T F) 3. Hetty called the doctor for her son.
(T F) 4. Hetty lived in New York.
(T F) 5. Hetty lived in an apartment with no heat.
(T F) 6. When Hetty died, she left $10 million.

iscussion

Discuss these questions with your classmates.

1. What famous person do you know of who had a bad characteristic? Say what he or she did.

2. Describe some other types of people who are not very nice, and say why.

3. Some people are stingy about some things but spend money on other things. Are you this way? Give examples.

Unit 12 Delicacies

Louise's Restaurant

SALADS

Snake Skin Salad - smoked snake skin slices over green salad with lemon dressing......................7.75

APPETIZERS

Fried Ants - delicious deep-fried ants...............................8.95
Fried Brains - delicious fried lamb's brains......................12.95
Egg Forty Years Old! - a true delicacy..............................95.00

SPECIALTIES

B.B.Q. Snake - cobra served with rice...25.00
Ant and Spider Burgers - a house specialty, with mashed ants and spiders and garlic................22.50

DESSERTS

Chocolate Ants - ants covered in dark chocolate......................6.00
Honey-Coated Termites - served with ice cream........................6.00

✔ Pre-Reading Activity

Discuss these questions.

1. Discuss the items on the menu.

2. Which ones would you want to eat? Why or why not?

Reading

Would you like some chicken feet? How about frog's legs? Well, you can't say no to a fifty-year-old egg! It's a delicacy that people pay a lot of money for, believe it or not. People in different parts of the world eat just about everything, from elephant's trunks to monkey's brains.

Chicken feet are a favorite appetizer in China, while in Taiwan turkey feet are a favorite. In Taiwan, people have both chicken feet and turkey feet in their salads. Whereas Americans like the white meat of a chicken, people in Taiwan prefer other parts of the chicken, like the dark meat and the inside parts. They often deep-fry the skin and serve it separately, along with the main meal.

Snakes and eels are delicacies in most parts of the world. In France and England, fish shops sell eels that are alive. In Asia, there are special restaurants for eating snakes. Everything on the menu is snake: snake soup, snake appetizers, snake main course, and snake desserts! When you go to the restaurant, the snakes are alive. You choose the snake you want to eat. Then the waiter kills the snake before your very eyes!

People line up in front of restaurants in Malaysia, Singapore, Thailand, and Indonesia to get fish heads. The restaurants prepare the whole fish, but people start by eating the head, which they believe is the tastiest part of the fish. So many people ask for fish heads that the price of fish heads is higher than the price of the best steak.

What about eating a fish that can kill you? The Japanese put their lives in danger every time they eat this delicacy. The fish is called the blowfish, and it is very poisonous. Although they know that they could die, they continue to eat it. Every year, the Japanese eat 20,000 tons of blowfish, and 70 to 100 people die from it every year.

Rats and mice are also a special food in some parts of the world. In China, people like rice rats especially. They clean and salt them and leave them in oil. Then they hang them to dry. These rats sell in the market for

Notes

l. 2: **delicacy** = a special food that is expensive or hard to find   l. 4: **trunk** = the long nose of an elephant
l. 5: **appetizer** = a small amount of food served before the main meal   l. 7: **whereas** = while   l. 9: **deep-fry** = fry something in oil, e.g. *tempura* uses deep-fry mothod   l. 12: **alive** = not dead   l. 14: **dessert** = the last part of a meal, usually a sweet dish   l. 17: **line up** = make a line of people waiting for something   l. 24: **poisonous** = causing death or illness

twice the price of the best pork. Farmers in Thailand and the Philippines also love rice rats. In Vietnam, mice from the rice fields are fried or grilled. In Spain, there is a traditional dish called paella, which is made with rice and pieces of fish. In the town of Valencia, this dish also has rat meat to give it a special flavor.

Insects like termites, ants, and bees are delicacies to many people. In Africa, people fight over termite nests. They eat the termites alive and say that they taste like pineapple. In India, people make the ants into a paste and eat them with curry. In Borneo, people mix ants with rice. They say that the ants give the rice a special flavor. In Australia, the native people drink ants. They mash them in water and say that the drink tastes like lemonade! And bees are delicious when you fry them. You just can't stop eating them!

(524 words)

Notes

l. 30: **pork** = meat from a pig   l. 31: **grill** = cook on metal bars over a fire   l. 35: **insect** = any small creature with six legs   **termite** = a small insect that eats wood   l. 36: **nest** = a place where insects or other small animals live and produce their young   l. 37: **paste** = a soft, smooth cream   l. 39: **native** = original to a land
l. 40: **mash** = crush food

Vocabulary

Complete the sentences with the following words.

> native   grilled   delicacy   alive   appetizer   dessert   pork   paste

1. People pay lot of money for a _____ like a fifty-year-old egg.
2. In some fish shops, they sell fish that are not dead but _____ .
3. Meat can be _____ over a fire.
4. Pig meat is called _____ .
5. In Asia, snake can be an _____ before the main meal.
6. The _____ people of Australia are the Aborigines.
7. It's nice to have a sweet _____ after the main meal.
8. Sometimes, people make ants into a _____ like a cream.

Looking for the Main Ideas

Circle the letter of the best answer.

1. People in different parts of the world eat ____.
   a. only frog's legs
   b. just about everything
   c. only legs, brains, and eggs
   d. mostly insects and snakes

2. In most parts of the world, snakes and eels are ____.
   a. delicacies
   b. only appetizers
   c. not found in shops or restaurants
   d. desserts

3. Insects are ____.
   a. good only with lemonade
   b. special in pineapple
   c. delicious to many people
   d. popular in Africa only

Looking for Details

Circle T if the sentence is true. Circle F if the sentence is false.

(T F) 1. In Asia, there are special restaurants for eating snakes.

(T F) 2. In Australia, they mash ants in rice.

(T F) 3. In India, people make ants into a soup.

(T F) 4. Some people say that bees are delicious when you fry them.

(T F) 5. In Africa, people say that ants taste like eels.

(T F) 6. Some people pay a lot of money for old eggs.

Discussion

Discuss these questions with your classmates.

1. Do you know about any other strange foods that people eat?

   _____

2. Did you ever eat a kind of food that was strange for you? What was it like?

   _____

Unit 13 Corn Flakes

✓ Pre-Reading Activity

Discuss these questions.

1. What do you eat for breakfast?

2. Do you like cereal? If so, what kind?

3. Why do people eat cereal in the morning?

Reading

Will Kellogg was born in 1860. He had no idea that one day he would change the way we eat breakfast. Will had little education compared to his brother John Kellogg. John was the chief doctor at the Battle Creek Health Center in Michigan, where mostly rich people went to eat healthy
5 food and recover their health. Will worked very hard at his brother's health center. He was the accountant and manager and did everything else his brother didn't want to do. He also helped John look for new healthy foods for his patients. They worked together, trying to make a new healthy bread for breakfast from wheat. They tried everything with the wheat; they boiled
10 it and then rolled it out flat, but nothing seemed to work.

One day, Will cooked some wheat, as usual, and then had to leave. When he returned, the wheat had become stale. He decided to put this wheat through rollers anyway. To his surprise, each grain of wheat came out as a flake. When he baked the flakes in the oven to get them dry, they
15 became light brown in color. After he tried this a few times, he produced wheat flakes without the stale wheat. He asked his brother John to serve the new breakfast food in the dining room of the health center. The patients ate the new breakfast food and loved it. It was 1894, and a new cereal was born.

Even after they left the health center, patients ordered bags of the
20 cereal. By 1895, John and Will were producing 100,000 pounds of flakes every year and selling each ten-ounce box for fifteen cents. John was not interested in taking care of this new food business and left all the work to his brother, as usual. Will continued to experiment with new foods for the next few years and came out with a new cereal made from corn——he called it
25 corn flakes!

One of the patients at the health center was a man named Charles Post. As he walked around the health center, he watched how the cereal was made. When he returned home, he started his own cereal company. By 1900, the Post Cereal Company was making $3 million in sales. About this time,
30 more than twenty other breakfast companies started in Battle Creek——all

Notes
l. 6: **accountant** = a person whose job is to keep or check a financial situation   l. 8: **patient** = a sick person who is under the care of a doctor   l. 10: **roll** = turn a rounded object over and over on something to make it smooth   l. 12: **stale** = old, not fresh   l. 16: **serve** = give people something, such as food at a meal
l. 18: **cereal** = a breakfast food made of grain   l. 23: **experiment** = try new things

making cereals. The Kellogg brothers were angry that other people were using their ideas and getting rich.

The two brothers started to argue about the future of their cereal. John wanted it to be part of his health center only, while Will wanted to start a cereal company. This argument turned brother against brother, and they stopped working together. In 1906, Will opened his own cereal company, called the Toasted Corn Flake Company, and started to sell corn flakes. By 1907, his company was producing 2,900 cases of cereal every day. Will increased sales of his cereal all the time, spending millions on advertising.

Will Kellogg and his son worked together in the company. But they argued a lot, and in the end Will told his son to leave. By 1948, the Kellogg Company had sales of more than $100 million. Will Kellogg made millions of dollars, but he continued to live a simple life. He lived in a simple two-story house and preferred to give most of his money to help others, especially children. In 1930, Will Kellogg had started the Kellogg Foundation to help children. Will Kellogg died in 1951, at the age of ninety-one. He worked until the end of his life at the foundation. His company had become the world's largest producer of ready-to-eat cereal as the result of an accident. People continue to eat cereals because all they need is a bowl, a spoon, some milk, and a box of cereal.

(636 words)

Notes

l. 33: argue = use words to show that you don't agree   **l. 39: advertising** = telling the public about a product or a service in order to encourage people to buy or to use it   **l. 44: prefer** = like one thing or person better than another or others   **l. 45: foundation** = an organization that is established to provide money for a special purpose

Vocabulary

Complete the sentences with the following words.

> cereal   argued   stale   experimented   patients   served   rolled

1. The people who went to the health center were _____ of Dr. John Kellogg.
2. To make the boiled wheat into a flat sheet, John and Will Kellogg _____ it.
3. At the health center, Dr. Kellogg _____ healthy food.
4. Will tried different things with the wheat; he _____.
5. Will baked the flakes to make his new _____.
6. Will left the wheat for a long time, and it became _____.
7. The brothers did not agree; they _____.

Looking for the Main Ideas

Circle the letter of the best answer.

1. Will Kellogg ____.
   a. found a new breakfast food by accident
   b. and his brother found a new cereal
   c. found a new way to make bread
   d. was a doctor
2. Will Kellogg ____.
   a. worked with Charles Post
   b. started his own cereal company
   c. and his brother started a cereal company
   d. invented wheat flakes
3. Will Kellogg ____.
   a. did not like children
   b. lived like a millionaire
   c. gave a lot of his money to help children
   d. lived in a mansion

Looking for Details

Answer the questions with complete sentences.

1. Where did Will Kellogg work?

2. What did Will cook to make the new cereal?

3. Who was Charles Post?

4. What did Charles Post do after he left the health center?

5. When did Will Kellogg start his own cereal company?

6. What did the Kellogg Foundation do?

Discussion

Discuss these questions with your classmates.

1. Why do people invent things?

2. What is your favorite invention? Why is it useful?

3. Make a list of some inventions you use.

Unit 14: The Persian New Year

✓ Pre-Reading Activity

Discuss these questions.

1. When do you celebrate the New Year?

___

2. How do you celebrate the New Year?

___

3. Most people celebrate the New Year on January 1. When do other people celebrate the New Year?

___

Reading

The celebration of the Persian New Year is a little different from other New Year celebrations. Persia is the old name for Iran. The Persian New Year is called *Nowrooz*, which means "new day." Celebration of *Nowrooz* started about 3,000 years ago. It is a big family celebration, and people return to their hometowns and villages to celebrate the New Year with their family and friends. *Nowrooz* begins on the third Wednesday in March, which can be between the dates of March 19 and 22 and is the first day of spring. It lasts for thirteen days.

People start preparing for the celebration weeks ahead of time by cleaning their homes. They wash their rugs and curtains, clean their furniture, and often paint the walls of their home. They also make or buy at least one set of new clothes for each person. They bake pastries and put seeds in a pot to grow into a green plant as a symbol of spring and new birth.

Weeks before *Nowrooz*, every household lays special things on a table to symbolize the holiday season, just as people in the West decorate a Christmas tree. Because seven is a lucky number, there are seven things on the table beginning with the Persian letter *seen* (the English "s"). The seven things on the table are *samam* (a Persian snack made of flour and sugar), *skeh* (a coin), *sabzee* (green vegetables), *sonbol* (a hyacinth flower), *seer* (garlic), *senjeed* (a dried fruit), and *serkeh* (vinegar). Other things are also put on the table, such as apples, sugar, cookies, candles, a mirror, and a bowl with goldfish. They say that if you look at the goldfish as the New Year comes, it will bring good luck.

Many people dress up as Hadji Firooz, who is a symbolic character of the New Year, just as Santa Claus is of Christmas. Hadji Firooz wears a red satin costume and has black makeup on his face. He sings and dances through the streets, telling everyone that the New Year is coming. Today, people see him in shopping malls, just as you can see Santa Clause in the United States or in Britain.

Notes

l. 10: **rug** = a small carpet   l. 11-12: **at least** = not less than, probably more than   l. 12: **pastry** = a sweet mixture of flour, fat, sugar, and water that is baked   l. 13: **symbol** = a sign or object that represents a person, thing, or idea   l. 15: **household** = all the people living together in a house   l. 27: **satin** = cloth with a smooth surface

First, on the last Wednesday before *Nowrooz*, people light fires in public places. This is when the celebration begins. Family members line up and jump over the fire. This is to bring light and happiness throughout the coming year. Children run through the streets. They bang on pots and pans with spoons to beat out the last unlucky Wednesday of the year. They knock on doors and ask for treats like candy, just as children do on Halloween in other countries.

Then, on the night before *Nowrooz*, the whole family gathers around the table with the seven dishes. The oldest person in the family stands up, gives everyone good wishes, and hands out fresh sweets, pastries, and coins. People spend the first few days of the New Year visiting older family members and other relatives. They give gifts and eat wonderful meals.

Finally, thirteen days after the New Year starts, families leave their houses and go outside to a park or somewhere by a river where it is cool and grassy. They have fun by playing games, singing, and dancing. They also have a wonderful picnic and eat and relax; this ends the *Nowrooz* celebration until next year.

(560 words)

Notes

l. 34: **bang** = hit something in a way that makes a loud noise   **pots and pans** = metal containers used for cooking   l. 35: **beat out** = remove something by hitting   **knock** = hit something, usually making a noise   l. 36: **treat** = a special thing that gives pleasure, like candies   l. 45: **grassy** = covered with grass

Vocabulary

Complete the sentences with the following words.

> symbol   pots and pans   at least   treat   pastries   household
> knock

1. A person buys _____ one piece of new clothing for the New Year.
2. It is usual to eat _____ during the Persian New Year holiday.
3. Candy or chocolate is always a _____ for a child.
4. Children go to a home and _____ on the door to ask for candy.
5. A goldfish in a bowl is a _____ of good luck.
6. During the New Year celebration, each _____ has a table with seven things on it.
7. To make a lot of noise, children bang on _____ with spoons.

Looking for the Main Ideas

Circle the letter of the best answer.

1. *Nowrooz* ____.
    a. starts on the thirteenth day of spring
    b. celebrates spring
    c. celebrates the New Year
    d. is celebrated differently in every country
2. For the Persian New Year celebration, people ____.
    a. lay seven special things on a table
    b. eat a lot of vegetables
    c. lay seven delicious dishes on a table
    d. have a Christmas tree
3. The celebration starts with ____.
    a. people visiting relatives
    b. fires burning in public places
    c. a picnic
    d. singing and dancing

Looking for Details

Use complete sentences to answer the questions.

1. When does the Persian New Year begin?

2. How long does *Nowrooz* last?

3. How many things are put on the table to symbolize the New Year?

4. What color costume does Hadji Firooz wear?

5. On the night before the New Year, who stands up and gives people pastries and coins?

6. Where do people go on the thirteenth day?

Discussion

Discuss these questions with your classmates.

1. Which holiday is the most fun and enjoyable?

2. Do you think we should have more holidays? Why or why not?

Unit 15 A Poem

✓ Pre-Reading Activity

Discuss these questions.

1. What fruit is in the picture?

   _____

2. If you were very hungry, would you eat it?

   _____

3. What is your favorite fruit? Why do you like it?

   _____

Reading

This is Just to Say by William Carlos Williams

I have eaten
the plums
that were in
the icebox

5 and which
you were probably
saving
for breakfast

Forgive me
10 they were delicious
so sweet
and so cold

(28 words)

> **Notes**
> **l. 4: icebox** = refrigerator, a place to keep food cold   **l. 7: save** = keep something for the future   **l. 9: forgive** = stop being angry with someone; pardon someone   **l. 10: delicious** = having a good taste

Vocabulary

Complete the sentences with the following words.

> forgive   delicious   saving   icebox

1. We put the food in the _____ to keep it cold and fresh.
2. The plums tasted very good. They were _____.
3. I don't want to eat the plums now. I am _____ them for later.
4. I'm sorry that I upset you. Please _____ me.

Understanding the Poem

Write complete answers to these questions.

1. Why did the speaker write the poem?

   _____

2. What did the speaker do that was wrong?

   _____

3. How does the speaker feel about what he did?

   _____

4. Would you forgive the speaker?

   _____

Recognizing Style

Work with a partner to answer the questions.

1. What tells you that this is a poem?

2. What do you notice about the writer's use of lines and of punctuation?

3. How is this poem different from a traditional poem?

4. What kind of patterns can you see in the poem?

5. Read the poem aloud. Mark the places where you pause. Compare your answers with those of your partner. Decide which reading sounds best to you.

Discussion

Discuss these questions with your classmates.

1. Did you enjoy reading this poem? Why or why not?

2. Is it important to read poems? Why or why not?

3. Have you ever written poems? When and why?

Supplemental Notes

Unit 1 Robots

l. 8: **the Smithsonian museum** = 学問の普及を目的に 1846 年にワシントン D.C. に設立された国立の機関 Smithsonian Institution の中にある博物館。
l. 17: **identify** =「認識する、確認する」
l. 24: **"difficult"** =「手に負えない」
l. 26: **M.I.T.** =「マサチューセッツ工科大学」 多くのノーベル賞を輩出しているアメリカ有数の大学。

Unit 2 The Shape of the Face

l. 21: **be easy to be around ~** =「~のまわりにいることが簡単だ、つまり気さくで近づきやすい」
l. 22: **be at one's best** =「その人の人生で一番良いときだ」
l. 25: **make decisions** =「意思決定を行う、何かを決定する」
l. 30: **stand out** =「目立つ、抜きん出る」
l. 43: **so did Picasso** = Picasso had this kind of face.

Unit 3 Killer Bees

l. 1: **Sao Paul** =「サンパウロ」
l. 10: **colony** =「(ミツバチ、アリなどの) 集団、群落、コロニー」
l. 10: **four times its old size** =「昔(ここでは初め)のサイズの 4 倍」

Unit 4 Celebrating Fifteen

l. 27-28: **a bouquet of flowers and blessings and prayers** = blessings and prayers は一つのフレーズとして取り扱われているため、a bouquet of flowers, blessings, and prayers というように 3 つの名詞として並んでいない。

Unit 5 A Folktale

l. 2: **famine** =「飢饉(ききん)」 天候の異変などが原因で、農作物の収穫が減り、食糧が不足すること。
l. 10: **That doesn't matter** = (主に疑問・否定文で)「問題ない、構わない」

Unit 6 Lightning

l. 5-6: **of all the people who die from lightning** =「雷に打たれて死ぬ人のうちで」
l. 10: **can be as much as 100 million volts** =「最高で 1 億ボルトまで高まることがある」
l. 11: **like a streak of bright light** =「明るい光線のように」

l. 12-13: **within a few millionths of a second** =「一秒間の数百万分の１もたたないうちに」
l. 20: **lightning rod** =「避雷針」
l. 21: **Benjamin Franklin** = アメリカの政治家、科学者、独立宣言書の起草者の一人。
l. 25: **Airplanes are not as easy to protect as buildings** =「飛行機は建物ほど守りやすくない」

Unit 7　Potatoes

l. 19-20: **All they had to do was to plant the potatoes** = The only thing they had to do was to plant the potatoes
l. 21: **feed one's family** = give food to one's family, support one's family
l. 24: **die of ~** =「～が原因で死ぬ」
l. 30: **stop A from ~ing** =「Aが～するのを止める」
l. 32: **his men** =「王の家来」

Unit 8　Right Brain or Left Brain?

l. 23-24: **have problems ~ing** =「～するのに問題がある」
l. 27: **prefer** =「何かと比べてそれよりは～するのが好きだ」　ここでは左脳が発達した人が数学や論理が好きなことをふまえ、それよりは芸術、音楽、文学が好きだというニュアンスがある。
l. 34: **mean that ~** =「～ということを意味している」

Unit 9　Louis Braille

l. 4: **infection** =「感染」
l. 12: **by age eleven** =「11歳までに」　by はここでは「～までに」という意味。
l. 14-15: **Captain Charles Barbier** =「チャールズ・バルビエ大尉」　フランスの軍人、闇の中で使うアルファベットの記号法の考案者。

Unit 10　Laws About Children

l. 8: **Inuit** =「イヌイット」　アラスカ北部やカナダ東部からグリーンランド島（大西洋北部にある、デンマークの自治領の島で、世界第一の大島）にわたる地域に住むエスキモーのこと。
l. 34: **illegal residents** =「不法滞在者」

Unit 11　The World's Most Unusual Millionaire

l. 5: **stingy** = 脚注参照 (p. 62)　cf. thrifty =「つましい、倹約している」
l. 22: **as the years passed by** =「年月がたつにつれて」　pass by は「過ぎ去る」
l. 29: **for free** =「無料で、ただで」という意味の熟語。
l. 30: **oatmeal** =「朝食用オートミール」　cf.（英）porridge

Unit 12　Delicacies

l. 3: believe it or not = 信じようと信じまいとの意から転じて「信じられないだろうけど」の意味。

l. 7, 8-9: white meat, dark meat = 鶏で言うなら、胸肉やささみは white meat、もも肉は dark meat。inside part とは砂肝やレバーのような内臓の部位。

l. 16: before your very eyes = 「あなたのまさに目の前で」 very は「まさしく〜だ」という名詞を強調する語。

l. 30: twice the price of the best pork = 「一番高級な豚肉の２倍の価格」

Unit 13　Corn Flakes

l. 13: to one's surprise = 「驚いたことに」
l. 14: flake = 「薄片状」
l. 29: sales = 「売り上げ高」 この意味の時は複数形。
l. 45: foundation = 「（基金寄付によって維持される）財団」

Unit 14　The Persian New Year

l. 26: just as Santa Clause is of Christmas = just as Santa Clause is a symbolic character of Christmas

l. 36: just as children do on Halloween = just as children knock on doors and ask for treats like candy on Halloween

l. 40: give someone good wishes = 「お祝いの言葉を言う、祝辞を述べる」

JPCA 本書は日本出版著作権協会（JPCA）が委託管理する著作物です。
複写（コピー）・複製、その他著作物の利用については、事前にJPCA（電
日本出版著作権協会 話03-3812-9424, e-mail:info@e-jpca.com）の許諾を得て下さい。なお、
http://www.e-jpca.com/ 無断でコピー・スキャン・デジタル化等の複製をすることは著作権法上
の例外を除き、著作権法違反となります。

▼本文使用写真クレジット
p. 7 左 © 時事 / p. 7 右 © 時事 / p. 55 左 © paul prescott / p. 55 右 © catwalker

CONNECTION 2
Pre-Intermediate Level

2015年4月10日　初版第1刷発行
2016年4月5日　初版第2刷発行

著　者　Milada Broukal
編著者　宍戸通庸／家口美智子

発行者　森　信久
発行所　株式会社　松　柏　社
　　　　〒102-0072　東京都千代田区飯田橋1-6-1
　　　　TEL 03 (3230) 4813(代表)
　　　　FAX 03 (3230) 4857
　　　　http://www.shohakusha.com
　　　　e-mail: info@shohakusha.com

装　幀　小島トシノブ（NONdesign）
本文レイアウト　クリエーターズユニオン（一柳 茂）
組版・印刷・製本　シナノ書籍印刷株式会社

略号 = 697
ISBN978-4-88198-697-4
Copyright © 2015 by Michiyasu Shishido & Michiko Yaguchi

本書を無断で複写・複製することを禁じます。
落丁・乱丁は送料小社負担にてお取り替え致します。